STEP-by-STEP

GEOGRAPHY

Transportation and Communication

Patience Coster

Illustrated by Raymond Turvey
and Pamela Goodchild

CHILDREN'S PRESS®

A Division of Grolier Publishing

LONDON • NEW YORK • HONG KONG • SYDNEY
DANBURY, CONNECTICUT

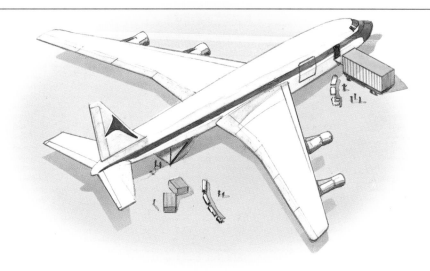

First American Edition by
Children's Press
A Division of Grolier Publishing Co., Inc
Sherman Turnpike
Danbury, Connecticut 06813

Library of Congress Cataloging-in-Publication Data
Coster, Patience.
Transportation and Communication/by Patience Coster;
illustrated by Raymond Turvey and Pamela Goodchild.
p. cm.--(Step-by-Step geography) Includes index.
Summary: Discusses how we move people and things by land, sea, and air, and
how we communicate through radio, television, satellite, and other means.
ISBN 0-516-20352-5
1. Communication and traffic--Juvenile literature. 2. Transportation--Juvenile literature.
[1. Transportation. 2. Communication.] I. Turvey, Raymond, ill.
II. Goodchild, Pamela, ill. III. Title. IV. Series
HE152.C85 1997   97-1979
388--dc21   CIP AC

Planning and production by The Creative Publishing Company
Design: Ian Winton
Consultant: Keith Lye

Photographs: Bruce Coleman: page 14 (Dr Stephen Coyne);
Mary Evans Picture Library: page 28; Robert Harding Picture Library: cover (C Moore),
page 5 (Jane Legate), page 7 (Gavin Hellier), page 13 (Bill Ross), page 18 (Charles Briscoe-Knight),
page 21, bottom (Adina Tovy), page 25, bottom (P Hattenberger), page 23, top; Image Bank: page 6
(J du Boisberran), page 10 (Andrea Pistolesi), page 25, top (G Heisler), page 26 (Max Dannenbaum),
page 30 (Andy Caulfield); Kia Cars (UK) Limited: page 31, top; Tony Stone Worldwide:
page 8 (Stephen Beer), page 11 (Joe Cornish), page 16 (Stephen Studd), page 17
(Will and Deni McIntyre), page 21, top (Sea King Rescue Team), page 27
(Hans Schlapfer), page 31, bottom (Walter Hodges);
ZEFA: page 12, page 23, bottom.

Contents

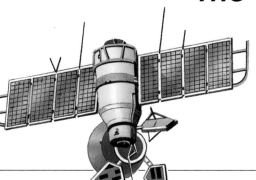

Traveling and Communicating

Look at this picture. How many
forms of transportation can you see?

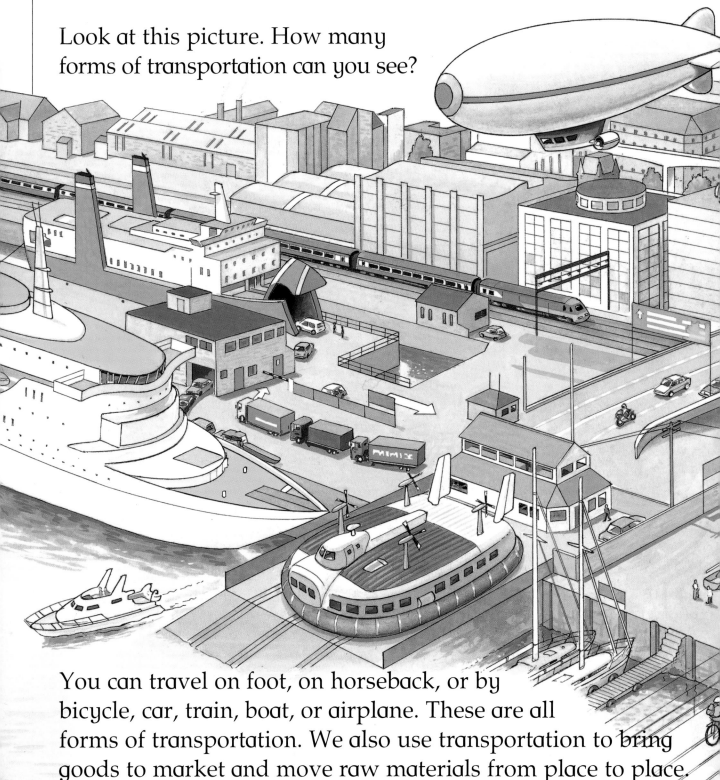

You can travel on foot, on horseback, or by
bicycle, car, train, boat, or airplane. These are all
forms of transportation. We also use transportation to bring
goods to market and move raw materials from place to place.

You don't have to travel if you want to stay in touch with people. You can write a letter or use the telephone. To stay in touch with the wider world you can listen to the radio or watch TV. These are all forms of communication.

Moving People

People have always moved from place to place. The first humans traveled on foot. Later, animals were used to carry people and pull carts. In the nineteenth century, stage coaches connected towns and cities across the country.

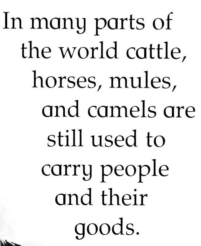

In many parts of the world cattle, horses, mules, and camels are still used to carry people and their goods.

The most modern forms of transportation on land are cars, motorcycles, trains, and buses.

On Your Bike

In Chinese cities you are as likely to see a bicycle as a car. Although they are much slower than cars, bicycles don't pollute the environment.

Moving Things

The transportation of goods throughout the world is as important as the transportation of people. On land, goods are carried by van, truck, and train. Barges move **freight** on rivers, canals, and lakes. Boats and tankers carry goods at sea. At the port below, containers are being loaded from a cargo ship on to a truck.

Airplanes carry mail and **perishable goods**. Heavy freight is costly to move by air, so it is usually carried by land or sea.

HOW IS OUR FOOD TRANSPORTED?

Look at the food containers in your kitchen. Which countries do they come from? What form of transportation do you think was used to carry each one?

Every day, letters and packages are transported across the world. Look at the pictures below. You can see the forms of transportation used to carry a letter from the United States to the UK.

1 The letter is taken by foot to a mailbox.

2 The mail is collected and taken to a post office by van.

3 The mail is then taken from the post office to the airport by truck.

4 It is carried to the UK by airplane.

5 A train takes the mail to a post office at a town in the UK.

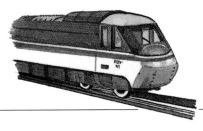

6 A postal worker takes the mail by bicycle to its **destination**.

9

Roads in Towns

Different types of transportation need different types of roads. Look at this photo and map of the city of Miami in the United States. What do you notice about the roads?

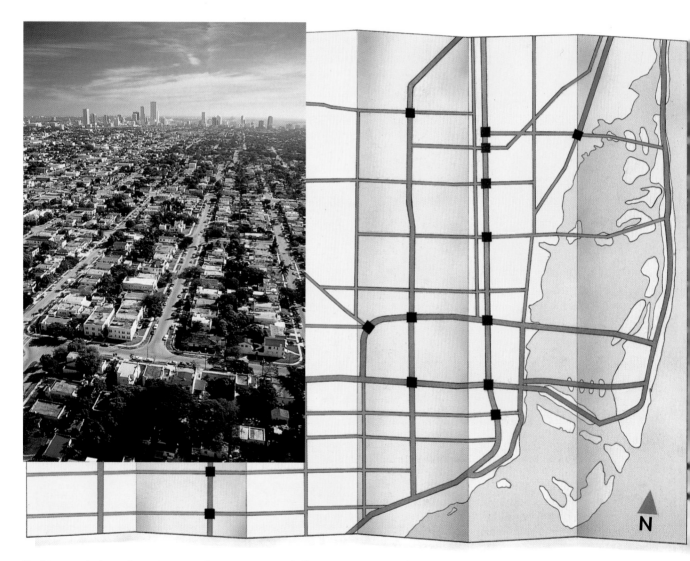

Miami is designed on a **grid** system, for people who want to travel around by car. The straight, wide roads enable traffic to move through the city quickly and easily. Cities like Miami have grown up over the last hundred years.

Look at this photo and map of Florence in Italy. How do the roads differ from those of Miami?

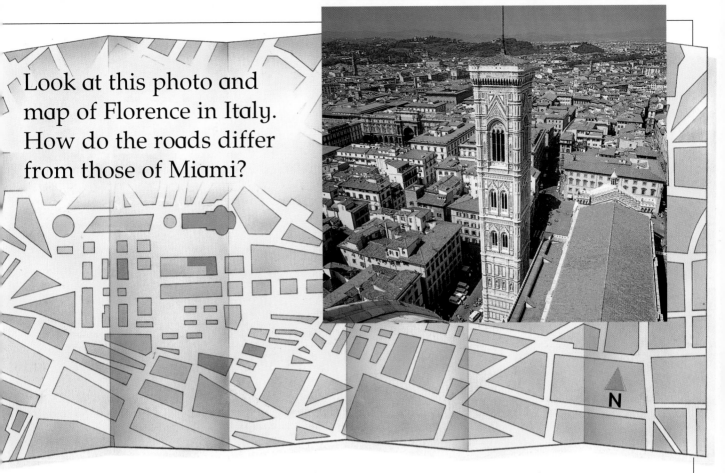

N

Cities like Florence grew up hundreds of years ago, before cars were invented. The short, narrow streets were designed for people on foot or on horseback.

SIGN LANGUAGE

Street signs are used to communicate certain things to road users. Look at these signs from around the world. What do you think they mean? Can you guess which countries they are from? The answers are on page 32.

1.   2.   3.   4.   5.   6.

Transportation by Train

Railroad tracks now criss-cross most countries in the world. Many people use local trains to travel to and from work.

Modern trains can travel great distances very quickly. The French TGV is the fastest train in the world. It can reach speeds of up to 175 miles per hour.

High-speed trains are a convenient and relaxing way of traveling between large cities.

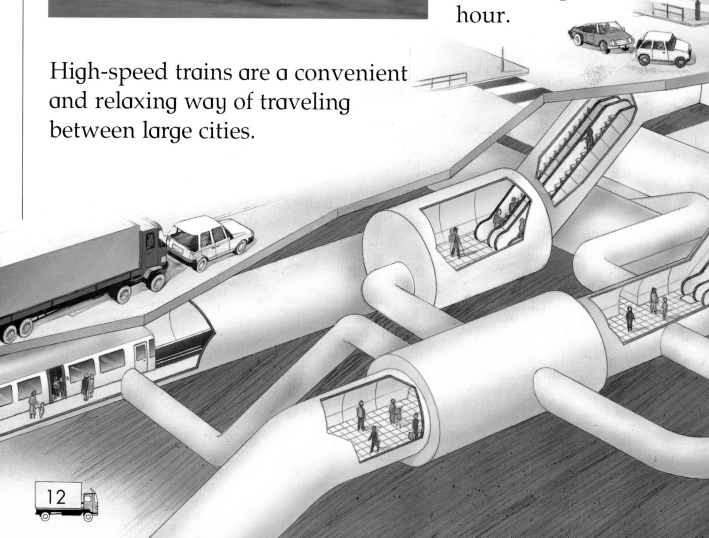

It is difficult building railroad tracks through cities, so they are often put underground. This way, people can travel around town quickly, avoiding traffic jams on the streets above!

City Railways

Monorail systems like this one in Sydney, Australia, are sometimes used in cities. The trains run on one rail above ground.

Bridges and Tunnels

A viaduct is a long bridge supported by arches.

What happens when roads and railroads come up against obstacles, like mountains and rivers? Look at the picture. It shows some of the bridges built to carry traffic across valleys, and a road tunnel going under a river.

This is a suspension bridge. The roadway is hung from chains or cables fixed to towers.

Swing It!

Some bridges, like this canal bridge in Amsterdam in the Netherlands, have middle sections that swing up to allow boats and ships to pass underneath.

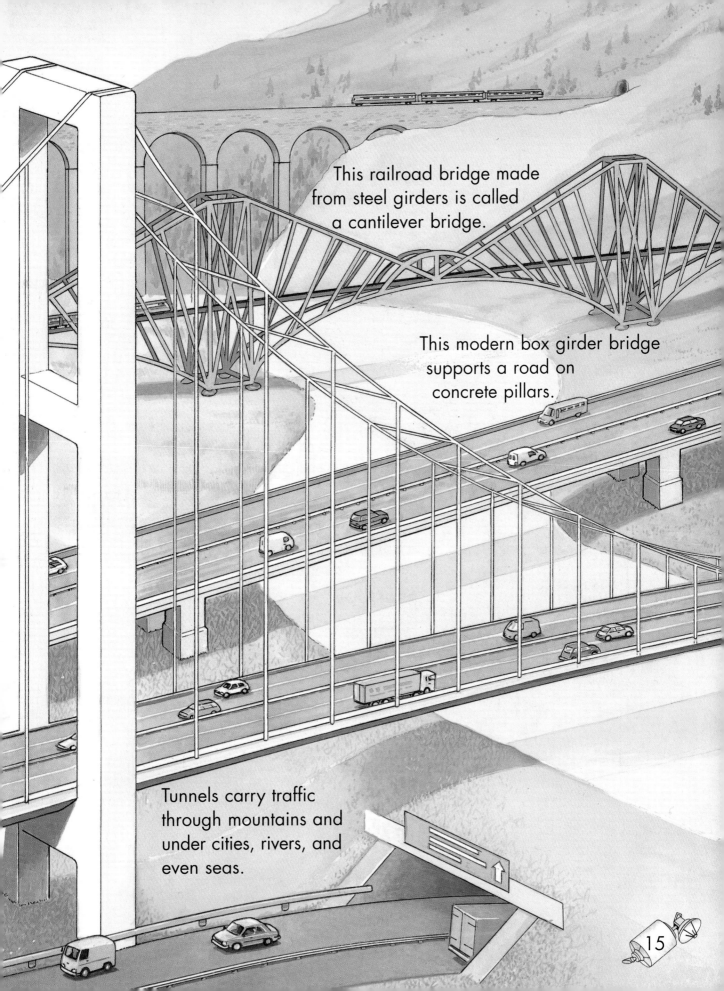

This railroad bridge made from steel girders is called a cantilever bridge.

This modern box girder bridge supports a road on concrete pillars.

Tunnels carry traffic through mountains and under cities, rivers, and even seas.

Rivers and Canals

Since the earliest times, people have transported goods and passengers along rivers by boat. This photo shows pleasure boats on the Mosel River in Germany.

However, people found that rivers didn't always go where they wanted them to. They dug new **channels** called canals. These usually ran from one town to another so that goods could be transported back and forth.

Traveling Through Locks

On canals, boats can be moved from one level to another using locks.

The boat enters the lock through gates, which shut behind it.

This ship is passing through the Panama Canal in Central America.

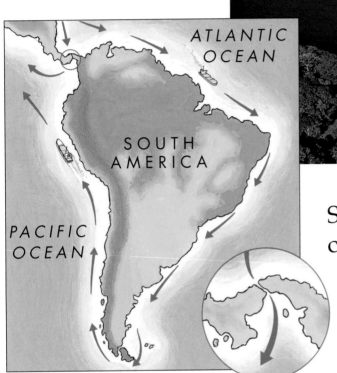

Ships can go through this canal instead of having to sail around the **continent** of South America. As the map shows, the canal saves thousands of miles of travel.

Water is let into the lock through flaps at the bottom of the gates.

When the water level has risen, the upper gates open and the boat leaves.

Sea Transportation

People use passenger ships, boats, and ferries to travel by sea from one country to another. Most of the world's heavy freight is also moved around by sea.

This tanker is full of oil from the Middle East on its way to a **refinery**.

This is a roll-on roll-off car ferry. The **bow** of the ship swings up to allow cars and trucks on and off.

This ship is loaded with grain.

Floating on Air

This hovercraft ferry carries people and vehicles. It floats above the land and water on a cushion of air.

This ship carries gas, which is pumped aboard through a pipe.

MAKE A HOVERCRAFT

1 Ask an adult to help you with this project. Cut the top section off a plastic bottle, ensuring that the cut-off edge is completely flat. Make a small hole in the bottle cap.

2 Blow up a balloon and stretch the neck of the balloon over the bottle cap.

3 Place it on a table and push gently. It will float over the surface of the table.

This cargo ship is loaded with containers. Each container is filled with goods.

By using sails as well as its engine, this cargo ship saves on fuel.

This is a cruise ship. People vacation on cruise ships around places like the Mediterranean and Caribbean seas.

Air Transportation

Have you ever flown in an airplane? If you have then you'll know how quickly you can get from one place to another. Aircraft are a very good way of traveling long distances.

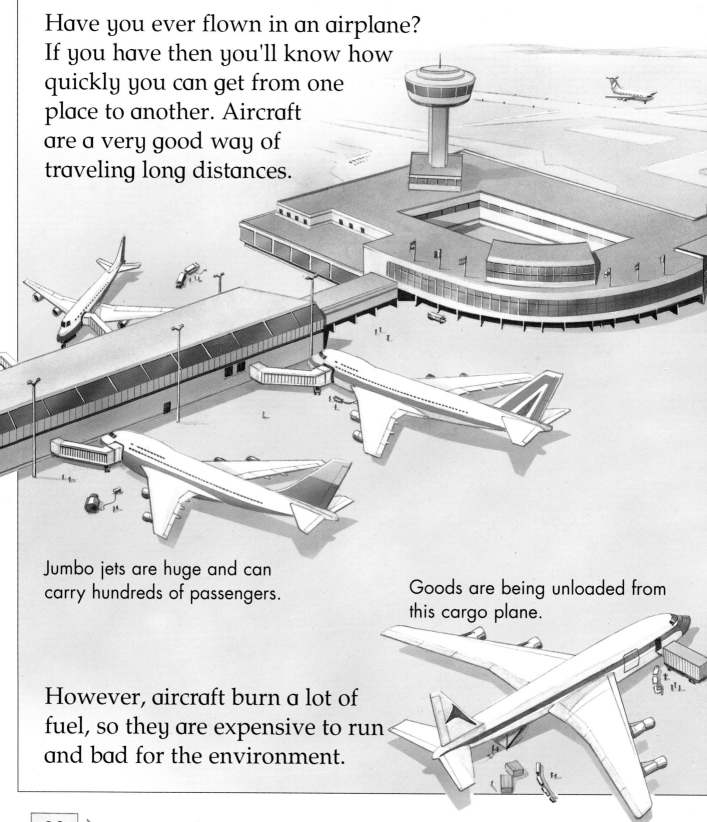

Jumbo jets are huge and can carry hundreds of passengers.

Goods are being unloaded from this cargo plane.

However, aircraft burn a lot of fuel, so they are expensive to run and bad for the environment.

Helicopters can take off **vertically**, so they don't need long runways. This helicopter is being used in a rescue operation.

These people are boarding a small passenger plane.

This mail plane carries letters and packages.

Hot Air Balloons

Hot air balloons were one of the first forms of air travel. Today they are used mainly for fun. The balloon is pushed up into the sky by air heated by gas burners. The passengers ride in a basket hanging underneath.

How We Communicate

Transportation is an important form of communication. But you can communicate with people without traveling to see them. Over the years, people have found many different ways of sending messages.

Some Native American people used smoke signals.

Sailors at sea used flags to send messages to other ships.

Just over a hundred years ago, the **telegraph** was invented. This enabled people to send messages along a wire to any destination in the world.

The invention of the telephone meant that people could talk to each other over great distances. Now we use telephones, faxes, and computers to send messages and keep in touch. They have become an important part of our working lives.

Optical fibers are strands of glass as thin as a hair on your head. Bunches of optical fibers are made into cables. A single cable can carry as much information as 10,000 telephone wires.

Radio and Television

Radio is a means of sharing information with many people. With a radio, you can listen to someone speaking into a microphone many hundreds of miles away.

Anyone with a radio **receiver** can hear the **broadcast**.

Information is also broadcast by television. The people in this photo are filming a TV program in a studio.

When the program is **transmitted**, our TV sets can receive it. TV sets receive both sound and pictures. The first televisions showed pictures only in black-and-white. Today, color TVs are commonplace.

Satellite Communications

Satellites are man-made objects that are rocketed into space. They **orbit** the Earth, sending and receiving information. Some send images of the Earth that are used to forecast the weather.

Satellites may be used for navigation, sending out radio signals that help ships and aircraft work out their positions.

Communications satellites are used to transfer telephone, radio, and television messages around the world.

1 Signal is beamed up from Earth station.

3 Earth station receives signal from satellite.

2 Satellite receives signal and transmits it.

Satellite Dishes

Earth stations that communicate with satellites use large, dish-shaped **antennae**. This Earth station is in Switzerland.

The Spread of Information

The invention of printing hundreds of years ago meant that the same information could be shared by many people. This picture from 1520 shows a printing press in Germany.

Printing used to be done by hand, but now books, magazines, and newspapers are printed by computerized machines.

How Newspapers Are Made

Newspaper reporters and photographers record the story.

Designers arrange the story on computer with the photos in place.

Today you can communicate with anyone anywhere in the world by computer. Books, newspapers, and magazines from around the world are available through the **Internet**. We can also order meals, do our shopping, and pay the bills through a computer terminal in our homes.

Large machines print millions of copies of a newspaper.

The finished newspapers are transported to the shops for sale.

The Future

For many of us, cars are essential to our everyday lives. But cars are bad for the environment. In towns and cities, where there is a lot of traffic, car **exhaust** gases **pollute** the air, sometimes causing a thick **smog**.

Exhaust gases not only poison the air we breathe, they also contribute to **acid rain**, which kills plants, pollutes lakes and rivers, and damages buildings.

Scientists are working on new ways to cut down traffic pollution. Less harmful types of fuel are being developed. The car in this photo is powered by the sun. You can see the **solar panels** at the back.

Today we are able to communicate with each other without having to travel. New communications systems mean that more people now work from home. Computers, faxes, and **videophones** have become part of our daily lives.

Glossary

Acid rain: Polluted water droplets in the air that fall as rain, sleet, and snow

Antennae: Devices used for sending or receiving electrical signals

Bow: The front part of a ship

Broadcast: A radio or TV program transmitted by electrical signals, or the transmission of a radio or TV program

Channels: Paths through which water flows

Continent: One of the large land areas of the Earth

Destination: The place to which someone or something is going

Exhaust: The used gases from a vehicle's engine

Freight: A load, or goods

Grid: A system of evenly spaced horizontal and vertical lines

Internet: An information system linking computers around the world

Orbit: To circle the Earth in space

Perishable goods: Goods that decay fast

Pollute: To make dirty or harmful to human, animal, or plant life

Receiver: A device in which electrical signals are turned into sound and pictures

Refinery: A place where raw materials are purified

Smog: Polluted air

Solar panels: Panels that turn sunlight into energy

Telegraph: A system that turns a message into electrical signals and sends it to a receiver

Transmit: To send out radio or TV signals

Vertically: Straight up or down

Videophone: A telephone combined with a TV receiver and transmitter

Index

Answers to questions on page 11

1 No sounding of horns (Nigeria)
2 Level crossing (UK)
3 Children crossing (USA)
4 Road works (UK)
5 Stop (Japan)
6 Wild animals on the road (Australia)